AF243900

When Teens Pray

Samantha Pegues

Copyright © 2016 by Samantha Pegues

All rights reserved.

No part of this book may be used, reproduced or transmitted in any form without written and signed consent of the author.

Published by: Pegues Enterprises

ISBN: 9780692588772

Unless otherwise noted,Scripture is taken from the *New Living Translation (NLT)*. Copyright ©1982 by Thomas Nelson, Inc.

Used by permission. All rights reserved.

Dedication

This book is dedicated to teenagers all over the world. You are awesome and amazing! God has great things in store for you!

"Don't let anyone think less of you because you are young. Be an example to all believers in what you say, in the way you live, in your love, your faith, and your purity."- 1 Timothy 4:12, NLT

Teens Rock!

Contents

Don't Sweat the Small Things

Ever flown in an airplane? When you're high in the air, the tallest people, buildings, and mountains look small. Did you know that your biggest problems are small to God? That big exam that you have coming up; the big argument that you had with your parents and the big fall out with your best friend are all small in comparison to God who lives within us. Worrying about your problems is equivalent to viewing them through a magnifying glass. Worry makes your problems seem much larger than they are.

I haven't seen over 90% of my high school classmates since graduation day. The big party that I thought I would die if I didn't attend, I could now care less about it.

The people and things that I thought were a major deal in high school; I can barely remember them!

Prayer: Dear God, thank you for being God. Forgive me for viewing my problems as more powerful than you. Forgive me for worrying about things that I can't change. Worry is a sign that I don't trust you. God, teach me how to cast my cares upon you. AMEN.

Memory Verse: "Don't worry about anything; instead, pray about everything. Tell God what you need, and thank him for all he has done." – Philippians 4:6, NLT

You can relieve yourself of unnecessary stress by remembering God's formula for your life:

GOD > my problems = TRUTH

What am I worried about?

____

____

____

____

____

____

____

What activities can I engage in to take my mind off of stress?

____

____

____

____

____

____

Get Back on Track!

Jonah disobeyed God by traveling into the wrong direction. Because of his actions, he was swallowed by a huge fish. Not only that, he traveled in the wrong direction for three days. Can you imagine that? However, Jonah made up his mind that he was going to be obedient to God's instructions and he headed into the right direction. Even though it seemed as if he was behind schedule, he still made it to the correct destination on time. Maybe you're like Jonah. Perhaps you've gotten off on the wrong start, and it doesn't look like you're going to finish school on time. However, if you make up your mind that you want to graduate on time, study harder, and do your homework, you still can finish on time even though you may be behind right now. What are you waiting for? Stop procrastinating! Get back on track! Finish strong!

Prayer: Heavenly Father, time is in your hand. Forgive me for procrastinating and not being a good steward of my time. Please help me to focus, get back on track and use my time wisely. Amen.

Memory Verse: "I have fought the good fight; I have finished my course. I have kept the faith:" – 2 Timothy 4:7, KJV

What has gotten me off track?

____

____

____

____

Who have I allowed to distract me from reaching me goals?

____

____

____

____

How can I get back on track? Example: Ask for extra credit or a tutor.

____

____

____

____

Me Against the World

Ever heard of the story of David and Goliath? David was a small shepherd boy who was chosen to fight a bully named, Goliath. Goliath was about nine feet tall, and he was mean and violent. Everyone in town was afraid of him. Can you imagine how David felt? He was only a teenager when he was chosen to fight the giant. However, David rose to the challenge, and he defeated Goliath with a slingshot and a small stone.

There are some situations in life that can cause you to feel afraid and alone. You may be hesitant to express your problems with your parents because they may not understand. You may even feel overwhelming pressure because they have been bragging to the world about how great and perfect you are. Confiding in your friends may not always be an option because they might view you differently. After all, you are supposed to be the strong and smart one.

What is your Goliath? A Goliath is anyone or anything that you're afraid to confront. Maybe it's going to college? Maybe it's teenage pregnancy? Or it might be a bully who's been threatening you with violence or posting negative things about you on social media? Don't fear! The biggest problems can be defeated with prayer, courage and just a small amount of faith.

Prayer: God, you are my world. There's no obstacle that's bigger than you. Give me wisdom and courage to face and overcome all my fears. Help me to let go of my pride and ask for help when I'm overwhelmed. Thank you for giving me the victory over all of my problems and enemies. Amen.

Memory Verse: This is my command—be strong and courageous! Do not be afraid or discouraged. For the Lord your God is with you wherever you go." – Joshua 1:9, NLT

Who or what am I afraid to confront? Why?

____

____

____

____

____

____

____

Describe a time when you were afraid? How did you handle it? How did God help you?

____

____

____

____

____

____

Nothing Can Stop My Success

Child abuse is a very touchy subject. However, it must be addressed so that you can overcome it. Otherwise, you may live your life in bondage to anger, rejection, promiscuity and you might even experience problems with your identity.

Child abuse isn't new, and it is not the end of your life. Moses' mother put him into a basket and placed it by a river. Yet, he became one of the greatest prophets ever to live. Joseph's brothers threw him into a pit and sold him to strangers. Yet, Joseph grew up and ruled an entire nation!

You cannot overcome abuse if you don't talk about it. Many teens hold on to abuse, especially sexual abuse, because they are too embarrassed to talk about it. Therefore, many of them become angry, violent, withdrawn, or begin to show changes in their sexual orientation. Ask God for wisdom concerning whom you should confide in.

Sometimes, it's your family who hurts you the most! However, you must forgive them so that you can experience emotional freedom and enjoy the life that God created for you. While parents are entitled to discipline their children, parents do not have the right to abuse them. It's important to remember that abuse is not your fault; neither is it grounds for suicide. You are not alone! Don't give up! God loves you! He has great things in store for you!

Prayer: Father, you are the perfect Parent! Thank you for the family that you have assigned me to. Touch their hearts and convict them if they even think about abusing me. Protect me from all forms of abuse. Abuse will not affect my mind, personality, grades, sexual orientation or destiny. I renounce every negative emotion caused by abuse. I will move forward and become a great leader. Amen.

Memory Verse: "Even if my father and mother abandon me, the Lord will hold me close." - Psalm 27:10, NLT

I forgive________________________________for abusing me. The abuse is not my fault. I am free. (Recite this statement every day until you no longer feel hatred, anger, hurt or guilt toward the person who hurt you).

How has abuse affected me?

____

____

____

____

____

____

What adult do I feel comfortable with confiding in? Why?

____

____

____

____

____

____

I Forgive You

Forgiveness is mandatory; not optional. Did you know that un-forgiveness can block your prayers from being heard by God? How can you sincerely pray to God out of a corrupt heart? If you aren't careful, you will hope for harmful things to happen to the person whom you haven't forgiven. It doesn't matter who hurt you, who lied on you, who abused you, or who molested you. If you want to see God, you must forgive them and love them; even if it means loving them from a distance. I know that it's easier said than done and it takes time. However, holding grudges causes you to become angry, bitter, and it can also cause health complications.

Most importantly, it can take you out of true fellowship with God. Sometimes, the hardest person to forgive is yourself.

Prayer: Lord, you are a forgiving God. Please remove all bitterness and hatred from my heart so that I can forgive the people who hurt and betrayed me. Yes, they hurt me, but I've also hurt you by not always being obedient to my parents. Yet, you repeatedly forgave me. There-fore, I don't have the right to hold a grudge because you never held one against me. Teach me how to forgive myself so that I might forgive others. God, please give me a clean heart that only does two things; loves and forgives. Amen.

Memory Verse: "If you forgive others for the wrongs they do to you, your Father in heaven will forgive you." -Matthew 6:14, NIV

What have I not forgiven myself for?

____

____

____

____

Who have I not forgiven? Why?

____

____

____

____

____

Who have I wronged and need to ask for forgiveness?
Apologize to them; even if they don't accept it.

____

____

____

____

Girl Talk

As girls become teenagers, their looks become a major deal. They begin to wear make-up, jewelry and they dress up to make themselves more attractive. Some overdress while others under dress by wearing clothes that are too short or fit too tightly. Many teenagers even display inappropriate behaviors by getting involved in sex, cursing, drinking, drugs or provocative dancing to get attention. However, none of those actions are necessary because God made you perfectly. God loves you just the way you are.

Think about it. Your brain, heart, and lungs are the most important organs in your body. However, they cannot be seen. Your heart is more important than your breasts, butt, and thighs. You would be in great danger if your heart was located outside of your body. The most
valuable things aren't advertised. God placed everything you need to obtain wealth and to attract a companion on the inside of you. Your body is priceless and should only be purchased with a wedding ring. Don't sell yourself cheap to boys who can only afford to shop clearance because they aren't willing to make a marriage commitment to you. Know your worth!

Prayer: Dear God, thank you for loving me just the way that I am. Teach me how to love myself. Help me to realize that my hair is gorgeous; whether it's straight, curly, kinky, long or short. My skin color and my body are beautiful just the way that you made them. God, teach me how to control my temptations with lust so that I can submit a pure body to my husband in marriage. Amen.

Memory Verse: "I will give thanks to you because I have been so amazingly and miraculously made. Your works are miraculous, and my soul is fully aware of this." -Psalm 139:14, GWT

Am I confident in who God made me? Explain.

____

____

Do I have to wear makeup to look pretty?

____

____

____

Do I dress to attract attention? Does the way that I dress attract negative attention?

____

____

____

____

Am I emotionally strong enough to be in a relationship with a boy without sleeping with him? (How do you know?)

____

____

____

____

Guy Talk

Adolescence can be a very difficult and frustrating time for teenage boys. During this time, there are a lot of hormonal and emotional changes taking place; in addition to boys trying to discover their identity in manhood. Often, teenage males attempt to establish their manhood through rebellion, violence, drugs, alcohol or sex.

Despite popular belief, real men don't sleep with a lot of women. They commit to one woman and only sleep with her after marriage. It's understandable to date more than one person during high school because it's a time when your personality and hormones are constantly changing. However, dating a person doesn't mean that you should sleep with them.

Many male teens endure unnecessary trouble by trying to establish their own identity instead of seeking God to find it. God created you and he knows you better than you know yourself. Society tends to label males who worship God as weak. However, that is totally false. Males can discover the strength and patience they need to abstain from sex, violence and drugs by developing a strong relationship with God. Teens can also receive revelation and direction from God regarding the right career path.

Prayer: God, thank you for creating me in your image. Forgive me for trying to find my identity in worldly things and people. Help me to understand that your Word is a mirror and it reflects who I am in you. Surround me with godly men who will help keep me on the right path. I will not pollute my body by sleeping with a lot of girls. Neither will I use alcohol and drugs as an attempt to appear to be manly. God, teach me how to love and respect my body. Amen.

Memory Verse: "God's will is for you to be holy, so stay away from all sexual sin." – 1 Thessalonians 4:3, NLT

People often act out to cover up their weaknesses. For example, people who have problems expressing themselves often curse or use violence as an attempt to cover up their weakness. Students, who struggle with understanding their school work, often disrupt class.

Make a list of your weaknesses.

____

____

____

____

How can I become stronger in the areas where I'm weak?

____

____

____

____

____

____

____

Getting Off to a Good Start

Nutritionists believe that breakfast is the most important meal of the day because it boosts your metabolism and gives you adequate energy for the day. People, who don't eat breakfast, tend to feel sluggish throughout the day and are usually easily irritated. They also seem to have higher cholesterol levels than those who eat breakfast.

Did you know that you consist of a body, a soul, and a spirit? It is essential to daily feed your soul and spirit with the Word of God. Spending time with God each morning helps us to gain the strength to calmly face daily obstacles in a positive manner. I have been able to refrain from anger and violence throughout the day because I had read about a similar situation in the Bible the same morning. While there will be times when you will lose your temper, or feel discouraged, beginning your day with God will definitely help strengthen you to conquer daily obstacles and give you more patience to deal with difficult people.

Prayer: Dear God, I cannot live without you. Your Word literally gives me life. Forgive me for not spending enough time with you. Make me hunger and thirst for you. Help me to crave your presence more than I seek to satisfy my flesh. Amen.

Memory Verse: But He answered and said, "It is written, Man shall not live by bread alone, but by every word that proceeds from the mouth of God." - Matthew 4:4, NKJV

7 Day Challenge

I challenge you to start your day with prayer. Read or recite at least one scripture before each meal throughout the day. Make a list of changes in your mood, appetite and energy level.

You Do the Math

Many teenagers aren't aware of the emotional damage that can be caused by having sex at a young age. Sex isn't just a physical act. Did you know your spirit and soul unites with the person you sleep with and every person they've slept with? That's why it's often so hard to let them go; even after you've broken up.

According to recent research, about three out of ten girls will become pregnant before the age of 20. That is equivalent to about 750,000 teenage pregnancies per year. Teen parenthood is the leading cause of teen girls dropping out of school. Approximately, fifty percent of teen mothers drop out of school. About twenty-five percent of teenage mothers have a second child within two years of the birth of their first child. Check this out! Did you know that eighty percent of teenage fathers do not marry the mother of their child? (www.cdc.gov; www.dosomething.org).

When you belong to God, you are not a statistic! You are an overcomer! If you already have a child, don't allow anyone to make you feel bad or look down on you for having a child. With the help of God, friends and family, you will become a great parent and have a successful career.

Prayer for teens who don't have children: Father God, thank you for giving me a healthy body. Teach me how to treat my body as the temple that you created it to be. Give me the courage, strength and patience to wait until marriage before I become sexually active. Help me to understand that it's privilege and an honor to remain celibate until marriage. Amen.

Prayer for teens who have children: Father God, thank for giving me free will to make my own decisions. Forgive me for disobeying your word. Teach me how to care and provide for my child while going to school. Surround me with people who are willing to help me move forward into a positive direction. Even though I was wrong for having sex out of wedlock, my child is a blessing to me; not a hindrance. I will finish school and become an amazing parent and leader. Amen.

Memory Verse: "Yet in all these things we are more than conquerors through Him who loved us" -Romans 8:37, NKJV

What could premarital sex cost me? What if I get pregnant or catch a disease?

____

____

____

____

____

Celibacy is unpopular to the world. Friends may walk away and you might not be invited to certain events.
What could celibacy cost me? How will I handle the criticism?

____

____

____

____

____

____

____

Stay In Your Lane

It's sad but we live in a world where people won't allow us to be ourselves. The world always makes comparisons. Is Lebron James better than Michael Jordan? Is Beyonce a better singer than Taylor Swift? I mean, who cares? They are all great at what they do. When people make comparisons, it can cause us to feel as if we are less than another person.

Comparing can also create jealousy and envy. Did you know that being jealous of another person is offensive to God? It's equivalent to saying, "God, I'm not thankful for what you've given me." God is the only person you should compare yourself to.

The media will lead you to believe that you should be a particular size, color or have a certain type of hair texture to be normal, handsome or beautiful. However, that's untrue. You are uniquely designed by God. You are perfect just the way you are. There is no competition when you're in your own lane.

Prayer: Dear God, thank you for my life. Teach me to keep my eyes focused on you. Help me to not be jealous and envious of the things that other people have. Jealously is a sign that I'm ungrateful for what you've given me. I am happy with and thankful for the gifts and talents that you've given me. Humble me if I look down on others who appear less talented as me. Amen.

Memory Verse: "A peaceful heart leads to a healthy body; jealousy is like cancer in the bones." – Proverbs 14:30, NLT

Who do I compare myself to? Why?

____

____

____

____

____

Make a list of characteristics that you like about yourself.

____

____

____

____

What makes me unique?

____

____

____

____

God Provides

Let's take a look at the story of Jonah from a different perspective. Jonah was disobedient to God's instructions. Therefore, he found himself trapped in the belly of an enormous fish. Although Jonah was in the belly of the fish for three days, the Bible never states that he was in any type of danger.

The fish's belly can be symbolic to solitary confinement. For teenagers, who may have a loved one who's incarcerated for disobeying the law, you can have peace in knowing that God can keep them safe even though they may have been disobedient and broken the law. While in the belly of the fish, Jonah wasn't employed. Therefore, he had no source of income to provide for himself. However, the Bible never mentions that Jonah was hungry or in need of any of life's essentials. Teens, who may have parents who are unemployed, can have confidence in knowing that God can supply all of their needs even though their parents may be going through a season of unemployment. During hard times, you do not have to commit a crime to acquire the things that you need. God will provide.

Prayer: God, thank you for being my Provider. Forgive me for not always believing in you. Even when I'm wrong, you are still willing to take care of me. Thank you for providing for my family and me during hard times. Protect those who are in prison and let them know that you are with them. Teach us how to prosper during times of economic hardship. Amen.

Memory Verse: "And my God will meet all your needs according to the riches of his glory in Christ Jesus."- Philippians 4:19, NIV

Make a list of things that God has provided for you and your family.

____

____

____

____

____

____

____

Write about a situation that you couldn't have made it out of without God's help. For example, a test that you didn't study for, an accident, etc.

____

____

____

____

____

____

____

Turn Up!

There's a popular phrase that is in circulation among teenagers. The phrase "turn up" means to get wild by partying, drinking or having sex. We live in a world that promotes sex, drugs, and alcohol. Teenagers, who choose not to participate in those activities, are often criticized and made fun of. While there is nothing wrong with hanging out and having a good time with friends, there are some things that you must learn to turn down; even if it means being criticized. It's better to be criticized for doing what's right than it is to be praised for doing wrong.

While having sex, or using drugs and alcohol may seem to be popular and may feel good for a moment, they could forever change your life in a negative way. Is it really worth it?

Prayer: God, you are an adventurous God! There is nothing boring about you! Give me the wisdom to teach my friends how to have godly fun. Help me to turn down sex, drugs, and alcohol. Teach me how to turn up my respect for my body. Turn up my grades, self-esteem, and boldness to stand for what's right; even when it's unpopular. God, I want to be all the way turned up for you. Amen.

Memory Verse: "But you are a chosen people, a royal priesthood, a holy nation, God's special possession, that you may declare the praises of him who called you out of darkness into his wonderful light." – 1 Peter 2:9, NIV

Make a list of fun activities that do not involve sex, drugs or alcohol.

How would you respond if you were asked to use drugs or alcohol?

It's My Life

Katie was a high school senior who had a strong desire to join the Air Force after graduation. However, her parents wanted her to attend nursing school to become a nurse because everyone in her immediate family worked in the medical field. Katie's parents began to pressure her into becoming a nurse. Consequently, she began to feel stressed, and she withdrew from her family. Katie didn't understand why her parents would try to talk her out of what she believed that God was calling her to do.

It's normal for parents to want their children to follow in their footsteps. There may even be times when parents are unable to recognize their children's gifts. In the Bible, Joseph's family didn't believe in his dream. David's father couldn't see that he would become a king. Parents must allow teens to follow the career path that they believe that God is calling them into; even if it doesn't work out. It will teach them to learn to distinguish God's voice from their voice. It's not always about being successful. Sometimes, God will use the experience to teach them a valuable lesson. God speaks to teenagers!

Prayer: Father God, you are my Life Coach. Give me clear directions for the career path that you have chosen for me. Teach my parents to not push me into a career that you haven't called me into. Open their spiritual eyes so that they will be able to see who you created me to be. Amen.

Memory Verse: "The LORD directs the steps of the godly. He delights in every detail of their lives. " - Psalm 37:23, NLT

Sometimes, a strong dislike for an area may be an indication of the career that God is calling you into. For instance, people who despise injustice are often called to be policemen, lawyers or judges.

Make a list of things/areas that you don't like?

____

____

____

____

Make a list of things that you do like. For example, list your favorite subjects, hobbies, sports and talents.

____

____

____

____

What career do you feel that God is calling you into? Why?

____

____

____

____

____

Words Do Hurt

Ever heard of the phrase, "Sticks and stones may break my bones, but words will never hurt me?" Well, that statement is false. Words can hurt; especially, demeaning and hurtful words that are spoken by someone you love. Verbal abuse often carries longer negative psychological effects than physical abuse.

For years, I worked at a psychiatric clinic for teenagers. One of the clients would have to be constantly restrained for cutting herself with sharp objects. One day, instead of restraining her, I sat on the floor beside her and had a heart to heart conversation with her. She explained that she cut herself to take her mind off of the horrible and degrading words that her mother spoke to her. She said her mother's words hurt her more than cutting herself with sharp objects! Can you imagine that?

Parent must be careful when telling their children that they're going to become like their relatives; specifically, when those relatives are not living a positive lifestyle.

Parents must also learn to refrain from calling their children ugly or stupid and from speaking curse words to their children. Some children are mentally strong enough to handle it, while others are not. Besides, according to Proverbs 18:21, life and death are in the power of the tongue.

Teens, it's imperative to know that God's words are more powerful than the words that are spoken by people!

Prayer: Father God, thank you for your prophecy over my life. I cancel every negative word spoken against me. God, turn every curse word spoken over my life into a blessing. God, you created me in your image; not my family's image. Therefore, I am a reflection of you. I am intelligent, loving, happy and successful. Amen.

Memory Verse: "For I know the plans I have for you," says the LORD. "They are plans for good and not for disaster, to give you a future and a hope." - Jeremiah 29:11, NLT

Always remember that you should never try to hurt yourself to take your mind off of negative words that were spoken to you.
What negative words am I holding on to?

____

____

____

____

Whose words have hurt me the most? Why?

____

____

____

____

What activities can I participate in to take my mind off the negative thoughts? For example, praying, singing, etc.

____

____

____

____

Rejection

Ever been rejected by someone you cared about? Maybe it was your family or friends? Or perhaps you were rejected by the cute guy from math class or the beautiful girl who chose to go the prom with someone else?

Rejection is so power but it's often underestimated. Once it takes root in your soul, it's not always easy to get rid of it and it often follows young people into adulthood. Common symptoms of rejection include rebellion, isolation, anger, depression, constantly lying, drug use and promiscuity. If a girl is repeatedly rejected by boys, she may seek attention and affection from another girl. The same is true for boys. Most people who suffer from rejection are easily offended and are very emotional. Do you feel as if no one likes you or that everyone is against you? Do you believe that everyone is racist? You may have a rejection issue.

Rejection often causes people to not only be afraid of failure; but they may be afraid of success as well. Many teens, who have rejection issues, have a fear of applying for college and they become content with working jobs that are beneath their potential. Most bullies also struggle with rejection. They seek to harm or degrade others as an attempt to reject others before they are rejected.

Is rejection affecting your life? Don't worry! You can be set free from rejection today!

Prayer: Father God, thank you for accepting me as your child. Help me to understand that I wasn't born to fit in with everyone. God, heal me from rejection and teach me how to love those who reject me. I renounce rejection, rebellion, bitterness, anger, promiscuity and every negative emotion that has entered my life because of rejection. I replace them with acceptance, obedience, love and purity. I am free! Amen.

Memory Verse: "The stone which the builders rejected as worthless turned out to be the most important of all." – Psalm 118:22, GNT

It's never acceptable to reject someone because of their race.

Who has rejected me?

____

____

Who have I rejected? Why?

____

____

____

How has rejection affected my personality?

____

____

____

Who accepts and loves me as I am?

____

____

____

____

Obedience Can Save Your Life

Because times are constantly changing, parents don't always understand the challenges that their teenagers face. Therefore, a disconnection can easily form between teenagers and their parents.

Parents, teachers, law enforcement and others who are in positions of authority are humans just like you. Their title doesn't prevent them from making mistakes. It's not uncommon for them to make comments that may make you feel embarrassed; especially at school where your peers may be watching and laughing. However, always respond to them in a calmly manner. Schools should be a place of safety. While teens' safety is important; the safety of teachers is also important.

It's significant to remember to never curse or act violently towards those in authority; even when they're wrong! If you feel the urge to act violently towards a teacher or a parent, ask to be excused and walk away. It's better to be punished for walking away than it is to receive a criminal charge for acting out of violence.

How to Handle Police Stops

Traffic stops can be very dangerous for policemen and citizens. When driving a vehicle, always keep your license and registration in a place where they can easily be accessed. If an officer pursues you, slowly pull over at the closest safe, well-lit area. If you are not close to a safe area, turn on your hazard lights, call 911 and report your location. Let the dispatcher know that you have a police officer behind you and you don't feel safe. Therefore, you are slowly driving to a safe location. After you stop, tell the dispatcher to stay on the phone with you. Have your license and registration in your hands before the officer approaches your vehicle. If your vehicle has tinted windows, let the windows down so that the officer can see inside of your car. Begin to pray for your safety! When the officer approaches your vehicle, make sure that your hands can be seen. Preferably, place them on top of the steering wheel with your palms up. Do not make any sudden moves and always ask the officer before reaching for anything. If the officer yells at you, take a deep breath and respond calmly. If you feel as if you have been wrongly accused, don't worry about it. Do not argue with the officer! Wait until your court date to argue your case.

I know that it hurts your pride when you must obey a person's disrespectful commands and endure unfair treatment when you've done nothing wrong. However, when you're involved in a dispute with law enforcement, it's best to swallow your pride and submit to their authority; even when they're wrong.

Obedience can save your life!

Prayer: Dear God, you are my Protector. Teach me how to respect those who are in authority; even when they're wrong. Soften the hearts of parents, teachers and law enforcement so that they might interact peacefully and respectfully to those who are under their leadership. Amen.

Memory Verse: "A soft answer turns away wrath, but a harsh word stirs up anger." - Proverbs 15:1, ESV

Pray for the President

Father God, you are the perfect Leader. Thank for the President who has been chosen to lead our country. Create in him a clean heart so they he will do what's right by all races and economic classes. God, we know that there might be hard times; but protect us and cause us to prosper during the times when the economy is down. Reveal unto us the plans of our enemies so that we will be properly prepared to defend ourselves against outside attacks. Turn the hearts of the leaders and citizens of this country back to you. Help us to love each other and bring peace between all races. We thank you that our country is moving into a new place; a place of peace, safety, prosperity and equal justice for all! God, make our nation great! Amen.

When Teens Pray, Nations Change!

www.ingramcontent.com/pod-product-compliance
Lightning Source LLC
Chambersburg PA
CBHW032248070726
47590CB00017B/3073